Think of Me

By

Apara Mahal Sylvester

Illustrated by Chrissy Chabot

Think of Me by Apara Mahal Sylvester

Copyright © 2021. All rights reserved.

ALL RIGHTS RESERVED: No part of this book may be reproduced, stored, or transmitted, in any form, without the express and prior permission in writing of Pen It! Publications, LLC. This book may not be circulated in any form of binding or cover other than that in which it is currently published.

This book is licensed for your personal enjoyment only. All rights are reserved. Pen It! Publications does not grant you rights to resell or distribute this book without prior written consent of both Pen It! Publications and the copyright owner of this book. This book must not be copied, transferred, sold or distributed in any way.

Disclaimer: Neither Pen It! Publications, or our authors will be responsible for repercussions to anyone who utilizes the subject of this book for illegal, immoral or unethical use.

This is a work of fiction. The views expressed herein do not necessarily reflect that of the publisher.

This book or part thereof may not be reproduced in any form, stored in a retrieval system, or transmitted in any form by any means-electronic, mechanical, photocopy, recording or otherwise-without prior written consent of the publisher, except as provided by United States of America copyright law.

Published by Pen It! Publications, LLC in the U.S.A.

812-371-4128   www.penitpublications.com

ISBN: 978-1-63984-026-7

Illustrated by Chrissy Chabot

This Book Belongs To:

_____

Dedication

To Sophie,

Always in our hearts.

Think of me when you are sad.
Memories of me will make you glad.

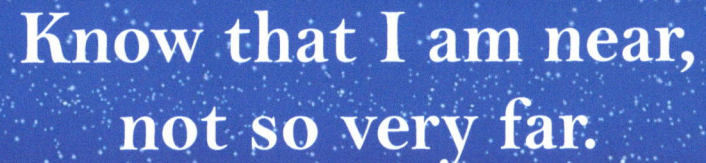

Know that I am near,
not so very far.

Think of me when raindrops sway.
Know that the skies won't always be grey.

Think of me on sunny days. As you lay outside and feel the sun's warm rays.

Think of me at Christmas, tree decorated in all its glory.

Remember me and my story.

Though I'm gone, remember dear,
my spirit is always with you,
always near.

In Loving Memory Of Mom

Think of me always and ever,

for my heart will be with you forever.

The End

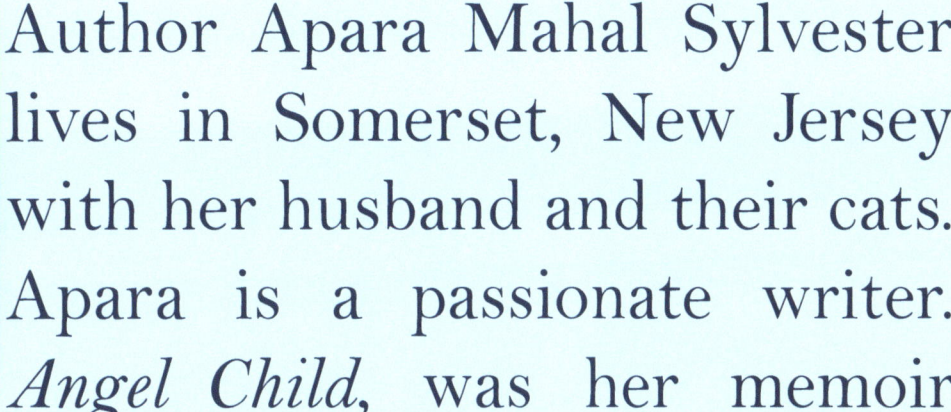
Author Apara Mahal Sylvester lives in Somerset, New Jersey with her husband and their cats. Apara is a passionate writer. *Angel Child*, was her memoir and was the beginning of her publishing career. See the next page for more books by this author.

Follow Apara on Facebook:

https://www.facebook.com/aparamahalsylvester/

Website: www.aparamahalsylvester.com

Other books by Apara Mahal Sylvester

Angel Child, a Memoir

Down By the River Where Dreams Come True

Cranky Frankie and the Lost Duck

Charlie the Baseball Cat

Lucy's Way Home

The Angel Tree

The Tale of Kitten and Ladybug

Chaplaincy: A Hospital Chaplain Intern's Journey

CPSIA information can be obtained
at www.ICGtesting.com
Printed in the USA
LVHW072021090323
741291LV00008B/106